Deeds of love

Gudrun Jane Limbrick

ISBN 978-1-903210-24-6

WordWorks
enquiries@wordworks.org.uk
www.wordworks.org.uk

Printed in the UK by 4edge Ltd.

The author has endeavoured to check all facts and provide full references where possible. All contact details were correct at the time of publication. The views given in the memories are those of each individual who supplied the memories. They are not necessarily shared by the author, the publisher or anyone else associated with this publication. It has not been able to check the veracity of the events and views given as fact within these memories. It is accepted that memories told in this way may be flawed and should not be taken as fact without independent verification.

Contents

Deeds of love

*"I have always had a great desire to do some deed of love
for the poor and helpless"*[1]

The Orphanage at Erdington was a remarkable building. Built by a remarkable man. The Orphanage, built in 1868 from three million bricks all made on the grounds, could be seen for miles around and could house up to 400 children in need[2]. To fund the project, Josiah Mason, a self-made man, gave his own fortune to the orphans including the house in which he was still living. Although he was not educated himself, and only taught himself to read and write as an adult, he created a school that was so good that not only were the orphans taught there, but local families were queuing up to get their own children in there.

But that is not the whole story. Josiah Mason[3] also laid the groundwork for the University of Birmingham and charitable works continue in his name right into the twenty-first century.

But are we in danger of forgetting what this man did? Mason's Science College has long since gone, Josiah Mason Street has gone, his home in Erdington has gone, his original almshouses have gone, even the Orphanage itself is long gone. The following pages use the memories of people who were in his Orphanage, or his school, and contemporary books and newspaper reports to look at the mark he has left on the place in which he made his home.

Looking after children

What to do with the poor, orphaned, or abandoned children in our communities has long been an issue in English society.

Of course, when our communities were rural and families worked on the land in small villages, the local community and extended family would take care of any children who were in trouble.

In 1601 this sort of help was formalised through the church[4]. A tax paid by local property owners was used by the church to provide for the community's poor. The church was able to give destitute families poor relief - a small amount of money - which would enable them to feed themselves until such time as they were able to take care of themselves.

Things began to change, however, with the Industrial Revolution. The population, growing hugely in number, began to move from the countryside into towns. Suddenly, local parishes were not just looking after the community that had been there all their lives, but large numbers of migrants, many of whom arrived in search of work but could not find any.

The dilemma was how to look after these people in London and other growing urban areas such as Birmingham. The answer was thought to lie in the workhouse. The paupers could be contained in these large institutions, fed and put to work to earn their keep.

Children in Crumpsall workhouse in around 1895

Erdington's first workhouse in the 1730s was by the village green where Erdington library now stands.

The workhouses were not popular and were seen as a last resort by people who had fallen on hard times. The plight of children in the workhouse was highlighted by one of our great social commentators, Charles Dickens, in the novel *Oliver Twist*[5]. He describes very clearly the hardship experienced by Oliver in the workhouse in the scene where Oliver dares to ask for more food.

Not only was the plight of children in the workhouse a cause for concern for some people but also the number of children living on the streets in the country's towns and cities was coming to the attention of philanthropists like Josiah Mason.

Josiah was not the only philanthropist who set out to help poverty-stricken and abandoned children.

Thomas Barnardo set up his first ragged school for street children in 1867. Thomas Stephenson set up his first children's home in 1869. Edward Rudolf set up a first children's home for 'waifs and strays' in 1881. These men, all based in London, were taking the first steps in what became three large organisations: respectively Barnardo's, National Children's Homes (now known as Action for Children) and the Children's Society. These organisations remain important agencies in child welfare today. Mason's Orphanage[7] opened its doors in 1868 - the year after Dr Barnardo set up his first children's home.

The cottage homes in Erdington were formally opened by the Guardians of the Poor in 1900 and could house 300 to 400 orphaned or destitute children at any one time[6].

As well as the work of these independent philanthropists, there was also a local authority response to the plight of destitute children in our cities. This mostly came in the form of setting up cottage homes—large institutions made up of small houses—run by each area's Poor Law Union. In most areas, the main role of cottage homes was to replace the workhouse as the place to which children were sent.

In what we now know as Birmingham , there were three sets of cottage homes for children - Marston Green in the west of the city, Shenley in the south and Erdington Cottage Homes just a few minutes' walk from Josiah's Orphanage in north Birmingham. Erdington Cottage Homes was opened next door to the workhouse by the Poor Law Union in 1900 - 32 years after Josiah opened his Orphanage. In several 'cottages' lining a quiet avenue, the cottage homes could house three or four hundred destitute or orphaned at any one time. While Mason's Orphanage closed in the 1960s, its near neighbour, Erdington cottage homes functioned until the 1990s.

It was not until after the Second World War that smaller, local authority and charity-run children's homes, coupled with fostering and adoption, began to look like the modern-day approach to looked after children.

Another local orphanage—Princess Alice Orphanage opened by the National Children's Home in New Oscott in 1882. The site is now a Tesco store.

Josiah Mason—the industrialist

So who was Josiah Mason and how did this Kidderminster man come to build an orphanage in countryside just north of Birmingham?

There are few publicly available pictures of Josiah as a young man. We will perhaps always picture him as he is here in his later years with his large white beard.

Josiah Mason was not an educated man, nor did he come from a wealthy or privileged family. He was very much a self-made man. To begin at the beginning, he was born in February 1795 in Kidderminster. His father was a weaver by trade and later became a clerk in a small carpet-making business[8].

For a time Mill Street in Kidderminster, where Josiah was born, was called Josiah Mason Street, but no longer.

Josiah had his schooling in the house next door to his family's home but left when he was eight to sell cakes on the street. He bought the cakes from the baker's and sold them door-to-door. He noticed that people paid in small change which was annoying for the traders so, enterprisingly, he began sorting and counting the coppers for these traders for which he charged a penny for each sorted pound. The next stage of his entrepreneurial activities was to get himself a donkey and panniers from which he sold fruit and vegetables.

When Josiah was about 15, he needed to change his mobile fruit and veg stall into a business he could carry on at home so that he could combine it with caring for his sick brother. He taught himself shoe-making by watching a local shoemaker and set himself up as a cobbler. He also taught himself how to write.

At the age of 19, he started work as a carpet weaver, following in his father's footsteps

At Christmas in 1816, Josiah made a visit to Birmingham, then a town of about 100,000 people, and stayed with relatives. He never went back to live in Kidderminster and the life of a carpet weaver.

The following year, he married his cousin, Annie Griffiths. They married in Aston Parish Church and moved to a house in Baggott Street. Josiah's uncle had invested his savings (from his job in a glassworks) in a gilt toy business and Josiah took on the role of running this for him. After several years, however, the business was sold and Josiah moved on.

It was during his time at the gilt toy business that Josiah must first have come to know Erdington. He was attending services at his local Wesleyan Chapel but also teaching at the Wesleyan Sunday School at Erdington.

Josiah then took a job with a split ring (the type of rings that are used to hold keys) manufacturer and lived in a house by the workshops. It was on this site that he eventually established his steel pen works.

Josiah worked in the business until the owner sold it to him for £500 in 1923. He paid the amount in instalments over the period of about a year. These split rings were very small things - selling for just a few pence each - but were to form the basis of Josiah Mason's fortune.

Split rings - Josiah's first venture into metalwork

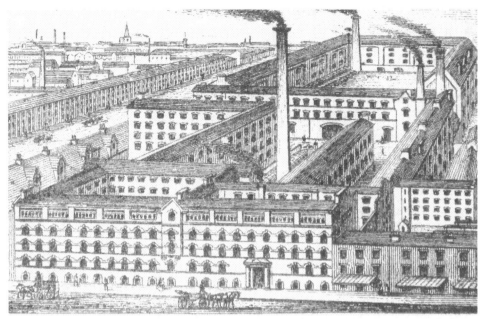

Josiah's steel pen works on Lancaster Street in the 1870s

Pen nibs were relatively new and expensive items at the time, although significant work had already been done in Birmingham on honing the manufacturing process. Josiah, seeing the potential, took a nib home to see how it might be made more cheaply. He did so very successfully and added nibs to his split ring business. He expanded the works at Lancaster Street and took on neighbouring land, and built more work space. At one time his steel pen works was the largest pen-maker in the world. Later, Josiah added electro-plating to his business empire with premises at Newhall Street.

It is perhaps ironic that a man whose lack of education meant that he had to teach himself to write, made his fortune by selling millions of pen nibs.

Above: a nib bearing Josiah's name

Left: a box of nibs produced by the Mason Steel Pen works and sold in conjunction with James Perry. The nib box, incorporating a real example of the nibs inside, was Josiah's own design.

11

Josiah Mason
- the philanthropist

After Josiah moved to Birmingham he lived in Aston and attended services at the Wesleyan Church in Erdington and took on the role of teaching at the Sunday School there. by 1851, he had moved to Chester Road. Ten years later, he was still in Erdington, on the Lichfield Road.

When Josiah knew it, Erdington was very much a place of growth. In 1824, it had a population of less than 2,000 people. In 1851, just 27 years later, the population had grown by nearly a third to 2,579 people in 442 houses[9]. Of course, while significant, this was nothing to the growth that Erdington would see once the railway arrived in 1862. By 1891, the population numbered almost 10,000[10].

Josiah was not immune to the poverty and displacement that comes with a growing urban area. He saw people begging and homeless and decided to do something about it. By this time, the self-made man was a man of significant wealth. His response was to build almshouses for older people and his first orphanage for children. He built on what was then called Sheep Street and is now known as Station Road in Erdington. Work began in 1858 when Josiah was 63 years old.

This first orphanage was built to take in 25 girls but was soon extended to double its potential capacity.

When Josiah was working on his orphanage and almshouses, Ann Mason was a member of the Fellowship of Methodists and, as such, was closely involved with the church which was without anywhere to worship in 1860. She suggested to her husband that he let them meet in the large entrance hall of his almshouses which were recently completed. Soon, however, the church was looking for more permanent

JOSIAH'S TIMELINE

1795	Josiah Mason born in Kidderminster
1816	Josiah arrives in Birmingham
1858	Almshouses and girls' orphanage open on Sheep Street
1862	Railway arrive in Erdington
1865	Foundation stone of Bells Lane Orphanage laid
1868	Work begins on building church on Sheep Street
1869	Orphanage officially opened on 31st July
1872	Josiah Mason knighted
1875	Foundation stone of Mason Science College laid
1880	Mason Science College opened
1881	Josiah Mason died
1890	Bunce biography of Josiah Mason published
1894	Erdington separated from Aston
1900	Birmingham University founded
1911	Erdington absorbed into Birmingham
1950	Orphanage school transferred to Birmingham Education Dept.
1952	Josiah's bust erected on Chester Road traffic island
1960	Mason's Orphanage closed
1961	Mason College closed (demolished in 1963)
1964	Orphanage buildings demolished
1974	Almshouses demolished
1983	Josiah Mason College established

premises of their own. Josiah once again stepped in to help. He leased the church the land they needed (at the bottom of Station Road, directly opposite the entrance to the station) and donated £100 towards the cost of the building. Reportedly, it is said that "architecturally, the church was very similar to the hall at the centre of the almshouses where they had been worshipping".

In the 1960s, there were still two Methodist churches in Erdington, one on Station Road and the other on the High Street. It was decided that they should replace both with one church that was big enough to serve both congregations. The last service in Josiah's church was in 1969. It was then demolished and a new church was built on exactly the same site. The new church opened in 1972.

The small orphanage on Sheep Street very quickly became too small for Josiah's needs, and he began to look for a suitable site for a new, much larger venture. When the new orphanage was built, the Sheep Street orphanage was converted into almshouses for 26 elderly women. On the site, on the corner of Station Road and Sutton New Road, now stands Osborne Nursery School.

The Methodist Church on Station Road was not the only Methodist Church that Erdington had. At the turn of the 19th century, another was built on the corner of the High Street and Newman Road. It has long since been replaced by Barclays Bank.

Josiah Mason's Wesleyan chapel on Station Road in the early twentieth century. Osborne School is on the left.

The Wesleyan Chapel in 2013. Osborne School can still be seen on the left of the picture, but everything else is very different.

Why Josiah decided to build an orphanage, in his own words:

"I am asked, 'How was it that you came to build an orphanage?' It was in this wise. I was constantly beset with beggars at home, in the road, the streets, and at my different works; and my head being constantly filled with business thoughts and plans, I found my hand in my pocket, to get rid of the intruders, and this at last happened so frequently that my pocket needed replenishing every morning. At last some cases occurred which led me to see that I was doing a foolish thing by indiscriminate charity.

"On one occasion, I remember that I met a blind man of decent appearance. This person stepped up to me, and said, 'Sir, this poor blind man has got employment at Liverpool, but has no means to take him there.' This appeal cost me half a sovereign. Next day, on my way to town, I saw the blind man and his companion both so drunk that they required a large portion of the road to toddle along.

"Another case. A woman came begging, on various pretexts, to one of my works. So well disguised each time and with such a plausible story, that I had no idea but that it was a different person on each visit. At last she came one day with one of her legs bound up , and said she had been discharged from the hospital incurable. She moved my compassion by describing her sufferings, with floods of tears. While she was there, one of the warehouse women came to me and said, 'Sir, I want to speak to you a minute. This woman (she said) has been here before in different guises; I am sure she is the same.' So I called the applicant into a room, and requested the warehousewoman to see the state of her leg. The effect was magical. Down went the leg and off like a shot went the beggar woman!

"Another woman came to beg some wine for a poor creature who, she said, the doctor declared must die, unless some stimulant could be given to her. I ordered some wine to be supplied. It was received with a thousand thanks, and with assurances that it would save the poor sufferer's life. I had occasion to go out directly afterwards; and there was the woman, the bottle to her mouth— held there closely until it was empty.

"Another, and a larger class of applicant troubled me. These were persons who required assistance to extend their trade, so as to put them in positions of comfort and independence. I advanced a great deal of money in this way; but found by experience that the good it did might be equal to 10 per cent of the money advanced; and that much of the remaining 90 per cent was wasted—too often in drink and idleness. These examples, - a few out of the many—put me on thinking that my spare money might be put to some better uses. I first thought of almshouses for aged women. 'Why,' I asked myself, 'not for men also?' but on reflection I concluded that they were not very well able to manage for themselves in such places. Then I thought of the orphans; and this brought me to a stand, to consider what to do. Finally I though 'Surely it must be some of each'; and having settled it so, I at once drew out a ground plan for an almshouse and orphanage combined-for twenty woman, and from twenty to thirty orphans. When the place was built and occupied, the orphans' claims became so pressing that I enlarged the place to make room for fifty girls; and more than this is it could not contain."

Josiah Mason, as reported by John Thackray Bunce, 1890[11]

Building Mason's Orphanage

The site Josiah chose for the new Orphanage was several minutes' walk from his original orphanage on Sheep Street. While the first orphans lived within the small town of Erdington, the new orphanage was further out in the adjacent countryside where there were very few buildings at all. This meant that there was scope for the Orphanage to have plenty of land - 13 acres in all.

The Orphanage was built using three million bricks each of which was made on the Orphanage's own land[12]. It was dressed with Tower Hill, Derbyshire and Shrewsbury stone. Josiah laid the foundation stone himself on 19th September 1865 in a quiet fashion without ceremony, but it took three years of building before the children arrived in 1868. The following year, on the 31st July 1869, the Orphanage was formally opened.

The building's architect, JR Botham of Birmingham, chose a design in the Italian style.

The key features of the building are the two towers which people must have been able to see for miles around. The smaller tower was a clock tower standing over the chapel, the second a ventilation tower which stood 150 feet tall. It was certainly a building which was built to be seen, and heard. It dominated the countryside surrounding it both in terms of the noise of its quarterly bells and the grandeur and size of the building.

Josiah spent approximately £60,000 on the building.[13]

If it were still standing now, Mason's Orphanage would surely have been one of the area's finest buildings.

Foundation dates of other significant buildings in the area

1400	The Lad in the Lane
1630	Pype Hayes Hall
1727	Rookery House
1730s	First workhouse in Erdington
1794	Oscott College
1822	St Barnabas Church
1848	The Abbey (the Church of St Thomas and St Edmund of Canterbury)
1868	**Mason's Orphanage**
1869	Workhouse (Highcroft)
1880s	Six Ways road junction
1882	Princess Alice Orphanage
1885	Jaffray Hospital
1900	Erdington Cottage Homes
1906	Erdington Library

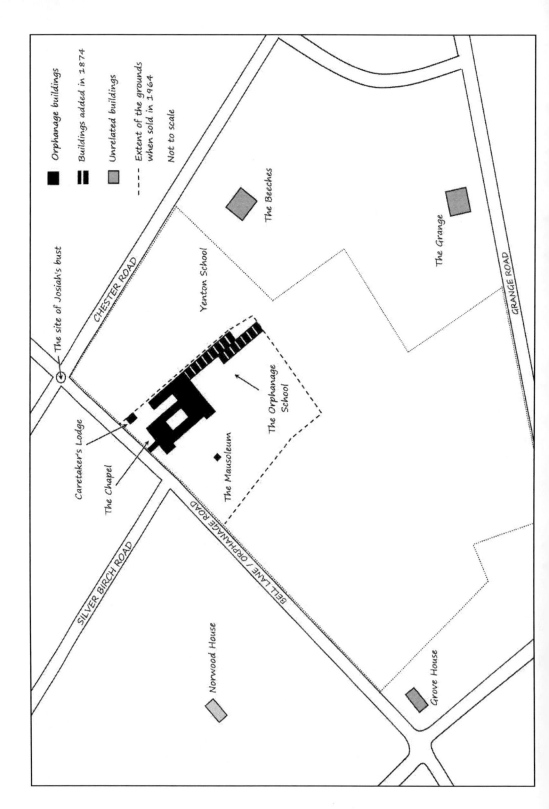

Legend:
- Orphanage buildings
- Buildings added in 1874
- Unrelated buildings
- Extent of the grounds when sold in 1964
- Not to scale

The site of Josiah's bust

CHESTER ROAD

The Beeches

Yenton School

The Grange

GRANGE ROAD

Caretaker's Lodge

The Chapel

The Mausoleum

The Orphanage School

SILVER BIRCH ROAD

BELL LANE / ORPHANAGE ROAD

Norwood House

Grove House

Early life in the Orphanage

It is accepted that life in the Orphanage was not easy for children. These young people who had perhaps experienced the death of one or both parents and a period of upheaval were brought into this large austere building without knowing anyone there or how long they might stay there.

It is likely that most would have been unfamiliar with their surroundings, as few originated from the immediate vicinity of the Orphanage. Visits from family members were often not possible because of the length and cost of the journey.

There were none of luxuries children might expect today. Children had few, if any, possessions of their own. Clothes were handed from one child to another and mended if they tore, rather than there being replaced with new clothes. The basics however - food, heating and running water - may have been a great improvement on what was available for some families living in the town.

Schoolwork in the Orphanage was taken very seriously and children were expected to undertake general housework including polishing the floors, preparing vegetables and cleaning shoes.

This description of the training of the girls comes from 1864 when the orphanage was still on Sheep Street[14]:

"The inmates hitherto admitted have been limited to girls, who, in addition to a sound English education, are taught such things which it is of importance they should know to fit them for the position of future wives of working men or as servants in families. With this in view, every girl is made practically acquainted with the art of baking, washing, and other domestic duties."

There was perhaps little affection between the adults working there and the children living there despite many of the children being newly bereaved and bereft of all they once knew.

A CERTIFIED MISTRESS REQUIRED for SIR JOSIAH MASON'S ORPHANAGE, at Erdington, near Birmingham.

Salary £60 a year, in addition to Board, Washing, and Apartments in the Orphanage.

Applications, with copies of testimonials, to be sent to the Secretary of the Orphanage before the 5th November next.

Candidates are requested to abstain from canvassing.

WANTED, at Sir Josiah Mason's Orphanage, at Erdington, near Birmingham -

UNDER HOUSEMAID. Wages £10 a year.
SEWING MAID. Wages £14 a year.
HEAD NURSE. Wages £14 a year.
UNDER NURSE. Wages £10 a year.
LAUNDRYMAID. Wages £12 a year.
UNDER LAUNDRYMAID. Wages £10 a year.

Application to be made to the Lady Superintendent, at the Orphanage.

WANTED. Immediately, at Sir Josiah Mason's Orphanage, Erdington, near Birmingham, a MAN and WIFE, under 40, without encumbrance. The Man to Take Charge of the Boys when out of School; and the Woman to Attend to Domestic Work generally.

Salary £43 a year, with Apartments, Board and Washing, in the Orphanage.

Application to made by letter, with full particulars as to age and previous occupation, to be sent to the Secretary, at the Orphanage, not later than the 1st November, 1881.

An advert in the Birmingham Daily Post
24th October 1881

Corporal punishment was not unusual in schools and children's homes at the time. Using a cane or a slipper was, unlike today, thought of as an appropriate means of punishment. And it was also thought, by many institutions, that bed-wetting could be effectively treated by punishing the child.

One luxury that the Orphanage did have for the children, even in these early days, was access to large sports fields and the children were encouraged to play all sports and spend a lot of their spare time outside in the fresh air. The site of the Orphanage was not what it is now, many houses and the bustling Chester Road, but a largely undeveloped rural area very much on the outskirts of the small town of Erdington.

An 1869 description of life in the Orphanage[15]:

At present there are about 160 orphans in the Orphanage, of whom 40 are boys. Their ages range from two years and a half upwards. The establishment consists of a matron, Miss Stockwin, a sub-matron and drill master, the elder girls acting as monitresses, a sewing mistress, and an out-door mistress. Great stress is laid upon the physical training of the children, and upon the industrial training of the girls, who do all the housework. The health of the children is placed under the care of two homeopathic practitioners — namely, Dr. Gibbs Blake and Mr. Wynne Thomas, both of Birmingham. The religious services in the chapel are conducted at present by the Wesleyan Methodists and provision is made for any residents in the

The Orphanage in 1869. Note that the school building has not yet been added. Instead the classrooms were within the main building.

neighbourhood who wish to attend, a special gallery, holding two hundred persons, being allowed to them. The friends of the children are allowed to visit them twice a year when Mr. Mason tells us, the place is 'like a fair' with the gifts of toys and the numbers of visitors. Friends are also permitted to visit at other times, on obtaining a written order.

Many of the children also no doubt had more food than they might have had if they had stayed in the family home and, for many, better access to healthcare. Sir Josiah was a great believer in homeopathy and each child's ailments were treated accordingly. The Orphanage did, however, like any such institution at the time, have to wage a constant battle against serious infectious illness. Scarlet fever, tuberculosis (known as consumption) and other diseases could all, if not checked, spread rapidly between children living in such close quarters.

The news reports below illustrate the concern about illness in the Orphanage and how the solution was decided to be the greater isolation of the Orphanage:

> *In consequence of the reported sudden increase of small-pox in Birmingham and neighbourhood, the trustees of Mr Josiah Mason's Orphanage have thought is advisable to give notice that the visiting on the 25th, 26th and 27th inst. will not be allowed.*[16]
> **1872**

> *At a meeting of the Aston Rural Sanitary Authority, held at Gravelly Hill Workhouse yesterday, Dr Bostock Hill (medical officer of health) presented his monthly report.—6 cases of scarlet fever at Sir Josiah Mason's Orphanage in the past month. (3 in the rest of Aston Union). He had made enquiries into the cases of scarlet fever at the Orphanage and found that the most likely cause of the introduction of the disease was the harvest festival held in the institution at which many persons were present from Birmingham and elsewhere. The festival took place five days before the first case occurred, this being about the average period of incubation of the disease. All the cases had been isolated in the cottage on the other side of the road. He suggested that, if possible, a small isolation hospital should be erected in the grounds of the institution sufficiently far away from the main buildings. If the present buildings continued to be used, he was of the opinion that a 7ft wall should be built enclosing the grounds.*[17]
> **1894**

One of the harsh realities of a nineteenth century orphanage—a graveyard for children who died during their stay was within the Orphanage grounds. See page 61 for more details.
Photograph taken by Benjamin Stone and reproduced here with the kind permission of Birmingham Archives and Heritage.

An early description of the orphanage building[18]

The Orphanage … occupies, with playgrounds, plantations, garden grounds, and fields, about thirteen acres of land, lying high on gravelly soil, well open on all sides, and commanding fine views of the surrounding country, from which its great central tower, 200 feet high, may be seen for many miles.

The plan of the interior arrangements is very simple. Access is gained from Bell Lane by a porch which leads to a lofty corridor, 121 feet by six, giving access to offices and staircases, and to various rooms in the south east front. On the left-hand side of the main corridor is a chapel, plainly fitted up with open benches. Beyond is a range of windows, looking into an inclosed courtyard. On the right-hand side of the corridor are a room, 37 by 30, for visitors, a board room for the trustees, and other apartments, including the private room of the matron. At the end of the corridor are a sewing room, 20 by 30, and a music and drill room, 30 by 37. Turning along the smaller corridor, we come to a dining room for the matron and teachers, a servants' hall, an infants' dining room (for there are a good many little ones in the orphanage), and then the main dining hall, 70 feet by 23 feet, fitted with massive tables, and with a separate seat for each child. Opposite the door of the dining hall is the kitchen, a superb room, 62 feet by 30 feet, well-lighted and lofty in proportion. All the cooking, it should be noted, is done by steam, on a most ingenious plan devised by Mr. Mason himself. Underneath, in the basement, is the oven for baking bread, of which, we need scarcely say, a large supply is wanted. This oven is also of Mr. Mason's invention, and is so constructed as with one firing to retain its heat for several days together, to the great economy of fuel. Opposite the kitchen, but divided from it by an open passage, is the laundry, fitted with all kinds of labour-saving contrivances, and having a series of very skilfully constructed steam drying closets. The whole of the steam required for these purposes, and the hot water for warming the entire building, through about 5,000 feet of 4-inch piping is supplied by one small boiler, with which is connected an engine for pumping water, hot and cold, to each floor of the building.

Ascending by a handsome staircase to the first floor, we find the general arrangements of plan similar to that ion the ground floor — the corridors corresponding and the rooms leading out of them to the several parts of the building. Amongst the principal are play room for boys and girls, a school room, three class rooms and thirteen small rooms allotted to various purposes. In addition to these are separate lavatories for boys and girls and so arranged that each child has its own washing place, towel and other appliances. Adjoining these is the wardrobe, fitted with separate hooks and places for the clothes of each child; and the bath room, a lofty apartment, supplied with an ample number of baths, and with hot water, contained in three iron cisterns. An important feature of the arrangements on this floor is the infirmary, which occupies a space in the entrance front, 47 feet by 30 feet, is capable of being shut off from the rest of the building, and has special means of heating and ventilation. Close to the infirmary is a convalescent room. The dormitories are situated upon the second floor, the whole of which is occupied by them. There are three for boys, the largest measuring 72 feet by

30, and the smaller ones each 23 feet by 18. For girls there are six dormitories, measuring 94 feet by 34 — the largest — down to 20 feet by 15, the smallest. The divisions are so arranged as to be capable of complete separation from each other; and in each division there are sleeping rooms for teachers or attendants, who have charge of the children during the night.

The principal staircase of the Orphanage drawn in 1869. The children appear to be being presented in their uniforms to visitors; perhaps the Trustees, local dignitaries or maybe even Josiah himself.

A gift to the orphans

In 1869, Josiah Mason relinquished formal control and ownership of the Orphanage and gave it to trustees making the Orphanage no longer one man's enterprise but a charitable organisation. Local newspapers lauded this in glowing terms as a great act of generosity[19]:

"A great work is best described in the simplest language. Therefore, without preface, we say that last Saturday witnessed the completion and dedication of one of the noblest works of charity in our time, or perhaps in any time — the transfer to the appointed trustees of JOSIAH MASON'S ALMSHOUSES AND ORPHANAGE, at Erdington, near Birmingham. By the desire of the Founder, a man of simple character and retiring habits, the event was quite unmarked by ceremony. There was just a quiet meeting of half a dozen gentlemen, the first trustees, at Mr. Mason's house, at Erdington ... at that quiet meeting a stately building, valued at £60,000, and a more than princely endowment, estimated at £200,000, the free and wholly unaided gift of one generous and large-hearted man, passed from private hands, and became the heritage of the orphan and the poor, for ever"

The trustees (who he said should be Protestant laymen living within ten miles of the Orphanage[20]) took on financial and legal responsibilities of the Orphanage. It was said that he did this to prevent the Orphanage coming under the 'control of any religious sect or party, or the funds being diverted from their proper use'[20]. While it still had the name of its founder, it was no longer *his* Orphanage. For the children, however, it probably made little difference. Josiah remained a neighbour and an interested presence in the Orphanage.

He not only gave the Orphanage to the public but he also ensured he gifted enough of his own assets to fund the work of the Orphanage into the future, namely:

- The buildings of the Orphanage and the land around it
- The almshouses
- Norwood House with 13 acres of grounds and gardens (making Josiah Mason himself a tenant in his own house and, as such, he paid rent to the Orphanage)
- Tyburn Farm (1023 acres)
- 1026 acres of other land including Nonsuch Farm in Northfield; Warkworth and Headless Cross Farm in Feckenham; the Chapel Fields estate at Bickenhill, Walmley Ash Farm and nearly two acres of land in central Birmingham in Broad Street, Great Hampton Street, Snow Hill and Summer Lane.

The value of this endowment was around £200,000 giving an annual income of around £10,000 for the Orphanage.

Initially, Josiah had tried to get donations from others but, in the main, his insistence that the Orphanage should not teach the Catechism, put off other donors. This was not because he was not religious but because he felt that 'religious difficulties' might hinder his work.[21]

The bells pictured during the demolition of the Orphanage

In March 1871, the bells were cast for the Orphanage clock. Josiah ensured that his new trustees had a lasting instruction from him. On the largest bell, in the centre of the picture above, he had the following written: 'I call upon the orphans' trustees to be faithful'.

The bells were cast, from metal from Josiah's own metal-works, by William Blews and Sons of Bartholomew Street, allowed to cool and then hoisted into position a few days later so that *"the inhabitants of Erdington and surrounding district may expect to be saluted every quarter of an hour with the chimes from the tower of Josiah Mason's splendid charity"*.

The Birmingham Gazette reported on the casting of the bells:[22]
"These bells, five in number, are composed of Mason and Elkington's pure deposit copper, with a slight admixture of tin. The large bell, which weighs 9cwt, will strike the hours, and the other four—respectively weighing 6, 5, 4 and 3 cwt—are intended to chime the quarters. The Orphanage clock, which regulates the peal of bells, and is now being constructed will have four dials, each five feet in diameter, three of which will be illuminated. The following inscriptions are on the Orphanage peal of bells: - Hour bell, 'I call upon the orphans' trustees to be faithful.' Four quarter bell, 'Josiah Mason, born February 23, 1795. Age 76, 1871.' Three-quarter bell, 'These five bells are made of Mason and Elkington's electro-deposit copper.' Two quarter bell, 'Timothy, chap. 3, verse 15.' One quarter bell, 'James, chap. 1, verse 27.'"

9cwt, the weight of the largest bell, is around 1,000lbs or 460kg. That is about the same weight as a horse.

The children of the Orphanage

Josiah Mason originally stated in the deed of the Orphanage that it should be for children from poor backgrounds who had lost both parents: *"every child shall be of or under the age of nine years, the legitimate child of poor parents, both then dead"*

This, however, changed relatively early on and children whose parents were living but could not look after them for a variety of reasons were taken in by the Orphanage. The proportion who were actually orphans began to decline. Some children had lost one parent, other families were perhaps struggling because of the illness of one or both parents.

One thing that Josiah Mason was very clear about in the deeds was that there should be no restriction based on the religion of the child or where he or she came from. It was perhaps in this spirit that, when *HMS Captain* went down in rough seas in the Bay of Biscay in 1870 losing almost all of the crew of 500, at least one child of the lost men was taken in by Mason's Orphanage.

The ship went down on 7th September 1870. The loss of the ship and nearly 500 men was devastating. It was reported that in just one street in Portsmouth thirty women lost their husbands in the disaster. On 29th September, the Ladies' Committee of the Portsmouth Relief Fund appealed for orphanages to take boys left without fathers by the *HMS Captain* disaster at reduced rates[23].

Mason's Orphanage responded to this appeal and, as a result, the first boy arrived from Portsmouth in November. It must have been a very difficult time for the boy, losing his father and getting used to a strange new home in a strange city all in the space of a couple of months.

The numbers and ages of children in the early years[24]

	Total number of children	Number of girls	Number of boys
1871	213	125	88
1881	316	196	120
1891	316	189	127
1901	289	159	130
1911	228	110	118

	Age range of girls	Age range of boys	Average (mean) girls' age	Average (mean) boys' age	Mode girls' age	Mode boys' age
1871	3—21	2 - 12	10.1	8.3	10	10
1881	4 - 16	7 - 14	11.1	10.7	11	12
1891	6 - 15	7 - 15	11.1	9	12	12
1901	4 - 17	7 - 15	11.1	10.5	14	11
1911	5 - 18	7 - 14	11.4	10.5	12	12

In the 1869 trust deed, Josiah Mason stated that *"the number of boys shall never exceed one -half the number of girls"*. However, the proportion of boys was already at 70% at the time of the 1871 Census and the number of boys had exceeded the number of girls in 1911. Josiah also decreed that boys could stay until they were 14 and girls until they were 18 if they had *"a bona fide intention of becoming teachers, nurses or assistants either in the Orphanage, or in other like situations"*. Even by 1911, this was still being largely upheld with girls being older, on average, than boys and some staying until the age of 18.

Place of birth of orphanage residents (by 2013 regions)[24]

	1881	1891	1901	1911
West Midlands	78.2	73.7	78.9	89.5
Erdington	0	1.6	1.7	3.9
Aston (excl. Erdington)	4.4	2.2	5.5	9.2
19th century Birmingham	32.9	40.82	48.8	48.7
2013 Birmingham	42.4	48.1	58.0	67.5
West of England	3.8	3.2	2.4	0.4
North West England	2.2	3.5	3.5	2.6
North East England	0.3	1.3	1.0	0
London	6.0	7.6	6.6	4.0
South East England	1.9	5.7	1.4	1.3
South West England	3.5	2.2	3.1	0.9
Yorkshire and the Humber	1.6	0.6	1.0	0
Wales	1.9	1.0	1.4	0.4
Scotland	0	1.0	0	0
Overseas	0.6	0.3	0.3	0.9
Not known	0	0	0.3	0

Number of children in the Orphanage [25]

When Josiah built the Orphanage, he saw a great need for a facility for a large number of children. Initially, the building was large enough to accommodate 400 children. In 1874, it was enlarged to accommodate 500. But the numbers of children never reached these levels. The 1915 annual report suggested that the trustees themselves were nonplussed as to why this might be:

"The average number of children maintained was 175, again less than that of the previous year. Under present conditions a reduction in numbers is somewhat surprising, but available information seems to indicate that this is the common experience of other similar institutions."

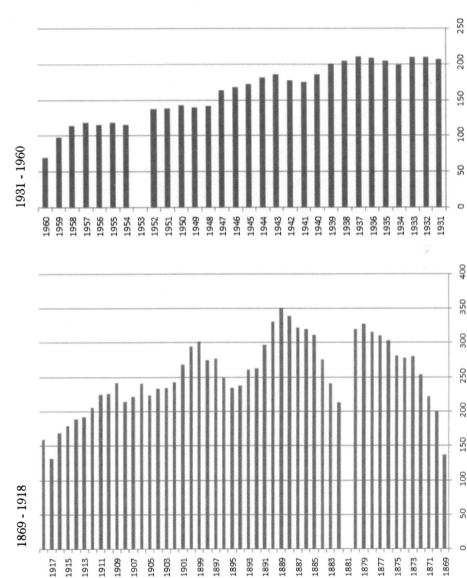

1931 - 1960

1869 - 1918

The Orphanage at the turn of the century:
Johanna's story

Johanna was researching her family's history when she discovered that three members of her family had spent time in Mason's Orphanage.

Johanna's great grand uncles were put in the Orphanage after the deaths of both their parents. Their mother, Jane, died on 6th September 1899 when she was aged 50. Their father, Michael, died two weeks later on 21st September aged 52.

The couple had had 22 children, 17 of whom had survived. After their parents' deaths, the three youngest children were all taken into care. Hugh, aged ten, and Leslie, aged eight, went into Mason's Orphanage on 15th November 1900. Hugh left in 1904, when he was 14 years old and Leslie left in 1907 when he was 15. Their sister, Elsie, went into the Royal Orphanage in Wolverhampton in June 1900 when she was nine.

Why their sister did not go to Mason's Orphanage with Hugh and Leslie, and where the three of them lived for the first year after their parents' death, we may never know. The 1901 Census does however, give us some clues as to what the boys might have found when they got to the Orphanage.

When the census was taken on 31st March 1901, the two boys had been at the Orphanage for four and half months, perhaps enough time to have begun to settle into their strange new surroundings.

There were 289 children living in the Orphanage - 159 girls and 130 boys[26]. Hugh and Leslie were used to being in a big family but this was on a completely different scale.

There were fourteen live-in members of staff: Alice Hawkins, the matron; two assistant matrons; two assistant schoolmasters; two assistant school mistresses; two accountant's clerks; a sewing mistress; a cook; a laundry maid and two nurses. Other staff members, such as the head teacher, may not have lived on site. The staff list suggests the importance given to education but also the practical issues of running a large institution with two accountants' clerks. However, looking through today's eyes, one laundry maid, one seamstress and one cook does not seem a large staff for nearly 300 children.

Hugh and Leslie are recorded as being eleven and eight respectively by the Census. That makes Hugh spot on the average age of the boys in the Orphanage at the time (there were actually 26 other eleven year old boys). Leslie, on the other hand, will have been one of the youngest boys there. There were only 18 other boys the same age as Leslie or younger. The boys will have attended the Orphanage school (at that time in a building adjacent to the main Orphanage building) and perhaps attended services in the Orphanage chapel.

At the time that Hugh and Leslie were there, one of the key events each year at the Orphanage was the Erdington Charity Sports Day. From 1897 this event, bringing together

Erdington Schools such as Slade Road School and Osborne Road School, was held in the grounds of the Orphanage *"for the benefit of large crowds"*. The Charity Sports Days were held in May of each year in the Orphanage grounds until at least 1909.[27]

The Orphanage at the time was based on a system of children sharing the workload. After school, each would have had chores to do around the Orphanage whether it be cleaning, preparing food, stoking the fires, cleaning shoes or another house-keeping task.

Incidentally, the census records that three of the 'inmates', as they were described, had formal roles within the Orphanage. 17 year old Lilian was listed as a pupil teacher while 15 year old Harold and 13 year old Alexander were office boys. Whether they were paid for this work is not recorded.

Hugh and Leslie were both born in Birmingham. Birmingham in 1901 was a very different place to the Birmingham we know now. It did not, for example, include Aston and Erdington as well as many other areas, such as Harborne and Handsworth which are now part of the city. It is thus unlikely that Hugh and Leslie were at all familiar with the area around the Orphanage. In all 141, children (49% of all the children in the Orphanage in

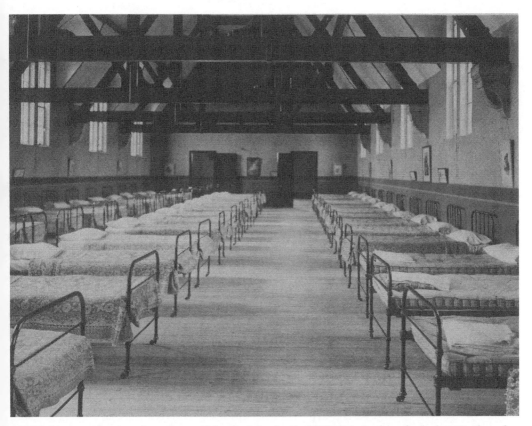

This photograph was taken of one of the dormitories in 1908. It is in these beds that Hugh and Leslie would have spent their nights at the orphanage. Photograph taken by Benjamin Stone and reproduced here with the permission of Birmingham Archives and Heritage.

1901) were born in what was then Birmingham.

After Hugh And Leslie's time (as can be seen in the table on page 30), residents of the Orphanage were becoming increasingly local ie. born in Aston and Erdington itself. In 1911, 4% of the children in the orphanage were born in Erdington, 9% in neighbouring Aston. If we look at modern-day Birmingham, 68% of the children in 1911 were born there.

What happened to Hugh and Leslie after they left the Orphanage in 1904 and 1907 respectively, is not known. Most commonly, boys went into apprenticeships, or joined the armed services as both options provided accommodation. Other boys may have been able to live with family members while they found their feet.

Chester Road, on the corner of which the Orphanage stood, at the turn of the nineteenth century.

34

The Orphanage school

Josiah Mason was not an educated man and it is said that he never read a novel in his life. Perhaps it was his own lack of education that meant that he placed huge importance on education and, specifically, on providing his orphans with an education. When the Orphanage was built, classrooms were set up within the main building. Initially, the school was for girls who were taught domestic duties which would have enabled them to take on work in service when they were older.

In his 1869 deed, Josiah Mason said that:
"Proper arrangements shall be made by the Trustees for the instruction of the children, having due regard to their respective ages and capacities in reading, writing, spelling, English grammar, arithmetic, geography and history and other such subjects of general and useful knowledge as many be, from time to time, directed or authorised by the trustees."

In 1874, the school was enlarged, housed in a new adjoining building, and began to take in both girls and boys from the Orphanage.

See page 57 for more on the history of the school.

A schoolroom in 1908, a photograph taken by Benjamin Stone
Image reproduced here with the kind permission of Birmingham Archives and Heritage

Sir Josiah Mason's death

Josiah Mason was knighted in 1872 by Queen Victoria. Eight years later he died. The last big act of Sir Josiah Mason was to lay the foundation stone of Mason Science College. The College stood on Chamberlain Square where the old 1970s-built Central Library was built.

While he saw Mason Science College built, he didn't see, and no doubt could not have envisaged, the large University of Birmingham it was to become.

He laid the foundation stone himself on his 80th birthday in 1875. In 1880 the college was opened and the following year, on June 16th, Sir Josiah died.

He died at his home in Norwood House, which he had built between Sutton Road and Orphanage Road in Erdington. He moved into it some time between 1861 and 1871. The house has long since been demolished and the site is now occupied largely by St Edmund Campion School.

THE ILLNESS OF SIR JOSIAH MASON.

Sir Josiah Mason, the founder of the Mason Science College, Birmingham, at a cost of nearly £200,000, and of the Mason Orphanage, at a cost of nearly £30,000, was yesterday lying dangerously ill at his residence, Erdington, near Birmingham. His medical advisers have abandoned all hope of recovery. Sir Josiah, who is over 80 years of age, began life as a mechanic, without a shilling.

A report of Josiah's illness 14th June 1881, The Huddersfield Chronicle

---

Norwood House stood between present-day Sutton New Road and Orphanage Road. It is said that he chose the spot as he could see the Orphanage from there. Of all his projects, it was his Orphanage that he wanted to be close to.

After the death of Ann, Sir Josiah's wife, in 1870, Sir Josiah had had a mausoleum constructed in the Orphanage grounds. While he was not to die for eleven years afterwards, the mausoleum, after the internment of Ann's body, had a place left for his own.

A description of Sir Josiah Mason's funeral from the Birmingham Daily Post[28]:

> *The funeral of Sir Josiah Mason took place on Saturday at Erdington. In accordance with the express directions of the deceased, he was interred in the vault in the Orphanage grounds where his wife was buried and over which he erected a handsome mausoleum to her memory. The proceedings, also by his express instructions were of the simplest character. The mourners consisted of a few relations and intimate friends .... And the only spectators were the children of the Orphanage, the inmates of the Mason Almshouses, and limited number of persons, most of whom were connected with the staff of the Orphanage of the Science College. The procession ... left Norwood House, the coffin borne of eight servants and workpeople. The route taken was by the private grounds attached to Sir Josiah Mason's residence, terminating at the small gate nearest the Orphanage, and thence along the high road. At the Orphanage the procession was joined by the elder inmates, consisting of about 150 boys and 200 girls.*

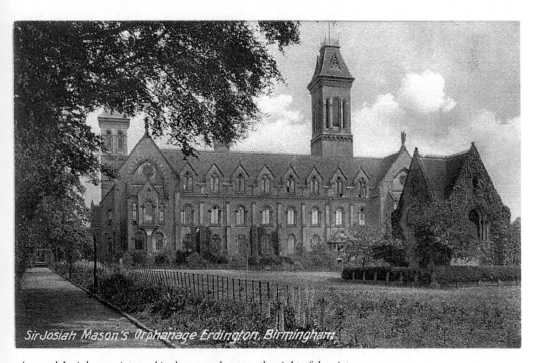

Sir Josiah Mason's Orphanage Erdington, Birmingham

Ann and Josiah were interred in the mausoleum on the right of the picture.

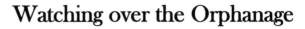

Watching over the Orphanage

In 1951, thirty years after his death, a bronze bust of Sir Josiah was placed on the traffic island junction of Orphanage Road and Chester Road at the instigation of the Erdington Historical Society of the time.

Sir Josiah faces not directly down Chester Road but his head is turned slightly so that he was looking at the Orphanage which was demolished thirteen years after the bust was placed there.

It has become a tradition to dress Sir Josiah's bust in a manner appropriate to the season by unknown people.

At Christmas, he is given a Santa hat, a St Patrick's Day hat on March 17th and he's even been known to sport an England shirt for the big football matches.

Here, he is dressed in red, white and blue in 2012. The note at the foot of the plinth reads:

'This statue has been yarn-bombed for the Queen's Diamond Jubilee and your pleasure by the Crochet Conspirators'.

The Orphanage Road bust is not actually an original. It was cast by William Blove from a marble statue which had been placed outside the Mason Science College building in 1885, a few years after Sir Josiah's death.

According to a contemporary news paper report[29], the marble statue was based on a cast that the sculpture, Francis Williamson, made of Sir Josiah's face after he had died.

The original seated statue can be seen on the bottom left of the photograph with the ornate building of the Science College behind it and the fountain on the right looking very much as it does today.

Below is a similar view of Chamberlain Square in 2013. In the place of the Science College is the former Central Library building (built in the 1970s) which, at the time of writing, is standing empty after the move of the library to the new Library of Birmingham building.

When Sir Josiah put forward his idea for the Science College it was not to discriminate as to who could get an education, and who could not. He was determined that it was to be open 'to the humblest artisan'.[30]

Parting Words

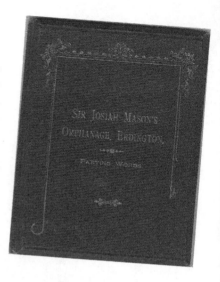

It was long the practice at the Orphanage to give each child the gift of a book when he or she left the Orphanage. The book had spiritual and practical guidance for each child and was based on the words of Sir Josiah himself.

The book pictured, Parting Words, was left by Pat's Great Uncle Harry. Pat tells us that Harry was seven years old and living in Walsall when he was orphaned after his mother's death in 1898. He was living in Sir Josiah Mason's Orphanage by 1901 although his younger brother was placed at St Michael's Home for Boys in Pelsall.

Harry was give the book when he left in 1904. In it, the words would have reminded him of Josiah's two great passions - religion and education. On religion, the book says this, and it is interesting to note that the children were not being encouraged to attend any particular church:

"The services that you have attended at the Orphanage have, I hope been a source of interest and benefit to you, and now that you have come to the time for leaving there, I trust you will regularly attend others in connection with some church or chapel where you can make yourself at home, and feel that you are likely to see spiritual good."

And the book would have reminded Harry of the importance that the Orphanage placed on education:

"...though you are leaving the Orphanage, your education is not completed. Nay! It is little more than begun; and it is the earnest desire of your best friends that while you throw energy and heart into your daily work and try to gain the character of good and faithful servants, you will devote much leisure time to the improvement of your minds, storing them with knowledge that will be useful in days to come."

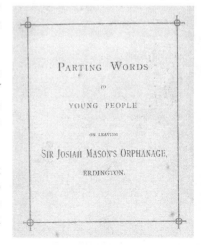

The book also made it clear that no one would be forgotten: *"Now that you are leaving your old house, I hope that you will not imagine that our interest in you will cease"*. The young people were invited to write letters to the Orphanage giving their news.

Harry himself went to work at another great Birmingham institution, Cadbury's, and later set up his own shop where he made boiled sweets,. The workings of that shop are now on display at the Black Country Living Museum.

An early picture of the Orphanage surrounded by farm land.

41

My earliest memories
Jim's story[31]

"As far as I can remember I was the age of three when my mother died and my father used to take me to work with him on his pushbike. One day he met somebody that advised him to have me put into an orphanage. He paid about a shilling a week or something like that to keep me in there. This was about 1923. We used to travel in a dickie seat car and go to a nursery at Six Ways because we were too young to go to the Orphanage school. That's my earliest memory. After that, we went to the Orphanage school.

"We had a uniform but that was only for Sunday best. Some Sundays we walked to the local church, different churches 'round about, and we all had a penny to put in the plate so they liked us to go. We had a playing outfit and a school outfit. When you came home from school, you had to put your playing outfit on.

"I think we got up at half past six in the morning. We had to make our bed., clean the dormitory before we down to wash and breakfast. Very keen on washing—the boys had a shower every night of the week before they went to bed. The shower was way down at the other end of the Orphanage school. At breakfast Mr Cleaver, the governor, would come into the dining hall and read out the news to us that was in the papers. 'This is what went on in the outside world', he would tell us. We would have chores, then another wash and then we would play until the school bell. You go to school until twelve. Before dinner you could play and then washed and up to dinner. Then you went to play again until the bell and school until four. Sometimes you had homework and you could go into the study rooms to do it. If not, you went and helped out in the kitchen until tea was ready."

BROADCASTING.

BIRMINGHAM 5IT (326.1 Metres)

3.0.—London Programme relayed from Daventry 3.45.—Station Pianoforte Quintet. 4.45.—Mr. S. Rogers; Topical Horticultural Hints—Wonderful Flowering Cherries. Winifred Firth (piano). 5.15.—The Children's Hour. **6.0.—Children's Concert relayed from Sir Josiah Mason's Orphanage. House Governor, Mr. Harry D. Cleaver, music director, Mr. J. H. Daniels.** 6.25.—For Boys'

The inclusion of musical broadcasts from the Orphanage was a common occurrence in the 1920s. This radio schedule is from 1927[32]. 5IT was a BBC radio station which broadcast from Birmingham, between 1922 and 1927

Greens in the stew
Enid's story[31]

"I went when I was about ten [in the 1920s]. The front passage was so beautiful because it had got these birds of paradise in frames and some of the big girls who were there had done lovely panels of embroidery.

"The first week I was there I cried. I cried every meal. Anyway, it got better and I got one or two friends and it was lovely you know. You can have fun - there's fun there that you don't get at home. There used to be a laundry with things you had to pull out to hang the washing in but you could sit in these and shove yourself in. We used to pinch cigarettes and smoke them—terrible we were. Then there were things like forbidden songs we used to sing—like 'Once I had a dark-eyed lover'.

"We used to have some lovely outings to Sutton Park to teach us about trees and that sort of thing.

"Then there was this porridge we used to have, and sometimes it was sour milk. And the thing was how to escape from eating it. They started putting our greens into the stew and when this was served up one day I found three crawly things, caterpillars, in it so I thought I'm not eating this so they said 'you are eating it and you shall have it for every meal until you've eaten it' so I sat at the head of the little boys' table but they brought me in a little piece of something for a bag and I used to put a bit of this stew in it and sneak it out of the dining hall until it all went."

The Town Gate entrance to Sutton Park

Famous Old Boys

Many many children passed through the doors of Mason's Orphanage and those children have gone to achieve many different things in life and take on many different lines of work. Some have achieved celebrity. While we don't know quite how many famous people began their days in the Orphanage, can be sure of two very famous (for very different reasons) Old Boys:

Horatio Bottomley[33]

Horatio was born in London in 1860. His father died when Horatio was just three, and his mother died six years later. Young Horatio was sent to Mason's Orphanage. He lived in the Orphanage until, when he was 14, he went to work as an office boy for a builder's form in Birmingham. He didn't stay long, however, and went back to London.

By all accounts, Horatio appears to have been a remarkable man. Starting as a court shorthand writer, he then went from one exciting business idea to another. Unfortunately, many of these landed him in bankruptcy. Undaunted, he decided on a political career and was elected as the Liberal MP for Hackney South in 1906. In 1921, Horatio ended up in prison, convicted of fraud in yet another of his business ventures.

Ronald Magill[34]

Ronald was born in Hull in 1920. His father died was Ronald was nine and he grew up in Mason's Orphanage. His mother went to Ireland where Ronald would visit her in the holidays.

After a brief stint as a tyre salesman, and his time in the armed forces in Word War II, Ronald began his acting career. While he had much work as an actor on stage and screen, he is best known for his role as Amos in *Emmerdale*, appearing in the soap from when it first started as *Emmerdale Farm* in 1972 and appeared in each of the 1970s, 1980s and 1990s.

EMMERDALE

Please drive carefully through our village

Like a big public school
John's Story

"I went into Mason's Orphanage in 1938 when I was eight. Prior to admission I can remember going in with my mother and we had a kind of interview. I remember waiting to hear that I had a place there.

"When we went in we were all given a number – I was 31 and you were known as your number, followed by your surname. I can still remember the numbers of my friends. Your number would be sewn into your clothes to identify them as being yours. I don't think I ever had so many clothes as we had then. We were all well turned out. We had best clothes, school clothes and play clothes. The rooms all had numbers as well – I can remember the boy's lavatory was Number 1: 'Number One, Number One, that's the place where we sit on!' The numbers were just one sign of the organisation of the Orphanage. It was run on militaristic lines.

"There were dormitories upstairs – the girls on the first floor, boys on the top floor. We had a large dining room with large tables that could seat thirty children. The younger children sat in the centre of each table with the older children at the ends. And it was the

The Orphanage looking down Silver Birch Road.

three eldest children who served out all the food – the less you served out, the more you had left for yourself. The ones in the middle of the table and late comers wouldn't get much.

"One person would be picked on to say grace. You never knew if it would be you or not. After breakfast there would be a bible reading and a prayer and some news so were kept well informed about what was going on in the War. At tea, there would be a talk by the Governor.

"These dining tables also gave us the opportunity for mischief – if all the boys pushed the table at once, we could dislodge the girls sitting at the other side and then pull the table back again before anyone knew what was happening. At one end of the dining room was a stage where shows were held. Outside there were extensive gardens which were worked on by two gardeners. They produced a lot of vegetables and fruit. Beneath the Orphanage were large cellars –it was in these that we slept during air raids.

"We had a sick room which had three wards leading off it and included an open-air balcony. The sick room was presided over by a uniformed nurse. When we had measles it was fantastic because many of us had it together. They would try to keep us apart from the others – I can remember we didn't eat with the others but used the dressing room for the swimming baths as our dining room.

"My Catholic background was forgotten in a non-conformist environment and I never went back to it. We all went to the non-conformist service on Sunday in the Orphanage chapel regardless of denomination. My mother lived locally in the Erdington area and she would come along as well. Often I would get to see her for a few minutes after the service.

"I think of the Orphanage as being like a public school really. We had houses like a public school. The children in the Orphanage were originally divided into two houses I think – Oxford and Cambridge but when I was there there were four houses – Jevons, Johnson, Tangey and Edwards – they were named after colleagues of Sir Josiah Mason. And we all gave each other (and the staff) nicknames like they do in public schools. The Governor was Pop. These nicknames were used more than the proper names.

"There was an emphasis placed on sports. And we were good at sports – but then what else was there to do after our school work and chores were done? We used to play against the other local schools and we'd usually thrash them. In fact, we won the Scouts sports so often that they said we could only enter every other year. We had a cricket square, not just a pitch but a cricket square. And it was mown all through the war years. Heaven knows where they got the petrol for that from! We would be well turned out for matches in cricket whites. There were many inter-house sports and the competition was fierce.

"A high proportion of us – maybe a third – got grammar school places. At times, the grammar school children were seated separately in the dining room because they had to leave earlier than the others. And they were also given fewer duties on school days. We made up for it at the weekend though.

"The other advantage of being a grammar school boy was that the Orphanage gave us three pence a week pocket money. I always felt like the odd one out at school though. I was never bullied but I felt we were different with our severe haircuts and we didn't have the freedom, home life and money that the other children had. Also, I was the only boy in short trousers in sixth form. We wore short trousers throughout our time at the Orphanage even thought this meant sometimes having long trousers cut down for us.

"Discipline was important in the Orphanage. There were maybe only half a dozen staff to look after us all so we took on chores. I scrubbed and polished a lot of floors in my time. We used bumpers and Ronuk polish. Ronuk was very important in our lives! The older boys were also given the job of disciplining the younger boys - the slipper was a common punishment.

"For more serious misdemeanours, the Governor would give the cane. I don't remember there being any injustice. Punishments were generally deserved. And odds on, if there were bullies they would get sorted by the boys. It was a very just place.

"Another job I was given was taking the sacks of shoes needing repair to George Payne in Kingstanding on the number 28 bus. This job gave us a great chance to escape. If we moved quickly enough we had time to go to the Pavilion to see a film before we'd be missed.

"Everyone of course had National Identity numbers then. My number ended in 110 and people would always say that I must have made a mistake because the end number showed where you came in the household – and how could I be 110th in my family? I was, of course, 110th in age in the Orphanage. There were two or three hundred children in the Orphanage when I was there. A big family!

"It being wartime, there was an influx of Jewish refugees while I was there. We didn't think anything of it and got to know them as we knew all the other children.

"I had to leave when I was 15 – that was a bind really. I had been expressed at school so I did get to spend one year at 6th. Children usually left after the School Cert.

"Looking back, I think I was there in a 'golden age' when life was good at the Orphanage with dedicated staff. I have heard that others coming along later did not always fare so well. I think the Orphanage equipped us to make the best of what we'd got. There were not many creature comforts but no real discomforts."

Sport in the Orphanage

As John's story, on the previous pages, describes, sport was very much encouraged in the Orphanage and school and it was played to the highest standards that they could manage encouraging competitiveness through, not only inter-house competitions, but inter-schools competitions too.

The Orphanage boasted large playing fields and these were used, not just for the benefit of the Orphanage and school but more widely.

For example, the annual Erdington Charity Sports Day, held on Whit Monday, took place in the grounds of the Orphanage with local schools such as Slade Road School and Osborne Road School coming in to take part. This event at the Orphanage started in 1888 and continued for many years.

The Orphanage also had a swimming pool and children were encouraged to compete in competitions with other schools in the area. For example, in 1921, the Erdington Swimming Club Championship was held in the open-air swimming baths at Brookvale Park. The Mason's Orphanage team narrowly beat the boys of Slade Road School[35]. The open-air pool was what we now know as Brookvale Park Lake which was used as a lido (or open air pool) from 1909 to 1927.

Final tables Erdington Schools' Football League 1931/32 Season - perhaps not one of the best years for the Mason's Orphanage Senior Team[35]

SENIOR A	P	W	D	L	F	A	Pts
Perry Common	14	14	0	0	74	10	28
Paget Road	14	9	2	3	51	42	20
Green Lanes	14	8	2	4	36	29	18
Ryland Road	14	5	2	7	42	48	12
National	14	5	2	7	31	34	12
Josiah Mason's	14	3	2	9	36	59	8
Moor End	14	3	2	9	22	52	8
Slade Road	14	2	2	10	26	48	6

An introduction to civilisation
Raymond's story

"I was in the Orphanage for about four years I think. I know I left when I was 15 so that would have been 1943. I really liked it quite frankly.

"My father died when I was very young and my mother married again. Before he died my two sisters had died before they were three – so it's a sad story.

"I was living with my stepfather in Derbyshire but it was all very crowded so I went to live with my mother's sister in Birmingham. She had her own daughter and we were all in a two -up, two-down so it was very cramped. So I was sent to the Orphanage by my aunt when I was eight or something like that.

"I was thinking about it just recently because I was writing my will and I said to my son that I might leave something to the Orphanage but he said that it had been demolished.

"I was good-looking then according to the Governor. Well the Governor was Mr Cleaver and then there was a Scots man who I remember had fought in the Boar War who was in charge of the older boys. This time we were all lined up for inspection and Mr Cleaver asked this Scots man who was the best looking boy. He answered 'I think Potter is'. I lived off that for a little while. I don't know why Mr Cleaver asked – he was a jovial chap.

"Was it strict? Well, I suppose it depended on who was looking after you. We had a sharp-tongued Miss Preece. She was always quick to get you into trouble.

"You had duties to do – doing the dishes and that sort of thing. Everything was highly polished – it had been built to a very high standard – so we had to polish the floors. You put on Ronuk and then two or three of us had the bumpers – a solid mop if you like – which buffed up the surface.

"We had to make our own bed, the dorm had to be cleaned. And I had a bit of bad luck. We had a sick bay and the matron asked the man who was looking after us to send a boy over to clean the sick bay. He turned to me and said 'off you go Potter'. It took me two hours every Saturday morning.

"We had a sports day with cricket, football and hockey. We had large grounds of course although with the War, on some of the fields the grass was dug up and food crops were planted.

"There must have been 240 children in the Orphanage when it was first built but the

numbers were diminishing. There were only 120 when I was there and a tiny group of very young children – almost babies.

"I did like it there. My family were such that they were dying off very rapidly so I was being shunted around. But my family was also a poor one – I didn't see a book! So the Orphanage was my introduction to civilisation. We had a library and a billiard table. And I loved sports.

"After I left the Orphanage I went to work for GEC and then I joined the navy."

The Orphanage in the Second World War

As Raymond and others remember, the War inevitably brought big changes to orphanage life. As part of the national movement to encourage people to grow as much food as they possibly could, some of the large fields were taken over for crop-growing although a sizeable sports field was still retained. Smaller children in the Orphanage were evacuated to more rural locations, such as Blackwell Hall in the Lickeys, although it was not possible to evacuate all children. As with Erdington Cottage Homes, many of the children remained in the Orphanage throughout the War.

The children in the Orphanage would have been subject to the same rationing as every other child, carefully managed by the kitchen staff. During the War, the Orphanage took in refugees. Many children's homes in Birmingham, and in other cities, saw an upsurge in the numbers of children they were taking in during the War years. However, as can be seen from the chart on page 31, this does not appear to have been the case with the Orphanage.

All the children were practised in the drill when the air raid sirens were heard and would stop what they were doing and run to their shelters.

One notable event of the War was that one of the barrage balloons tethered on Pype Hayes Park came free and blew over the Orphanage. It hit the clock tower causing some significant damage and creating a gaping hole in the roof.

What would have happened to me?
Ken's story

"I went into the Orphanage on 20th February 1939 when I was six years old. I went in with my older brother and sister and my younger brother. I can remember standing there at the gate and looking upwards at this huge building. I was holding my brothers' and my sister's hands and, as a six year old, I was frightened to death.

Before we'd arrived here, we'd been in a children's home called Summerhill House. It felt like we had been there an eternity but I think it was probably about six or eight weeks. We had had a terrible time there. As far as we knew, we had no family members, this was it for us. Being orphaned was an absolutely traumatic experience.

"The door of the Orphanage opened and we were ushered in and told to stand at the end of the long corridor which was lined with glass cases full of stuffed animals.

"After a little while, one of the staff held out a hand to me. Not used to this, I wondered what I had done to offend. But I needn't have worried for she was kindness itself. She was the matron, Mrs Cleaver. Together with her husband, and her three children, she ran the orphanage. This wonderful family could be very strict, but they were fair.

Summer Hill House

Ken went to Summer Hill House before being sent to the Orphanage. This was not unusual. Summer Hill, on Summer Hill Terrace was a receiving home run by the Birmingham Board of Guardians from 1905. As a receiving home, children stayed there for a few weeks until a permanent placement could be found for them in one of the children's homes in the city run by the Guardians or one, like Josiah Mason's which was independent. In 1939, the children living there were evacuated (it was very close to the city centre) and the home never reopened.

"She took me upstairs to what was called the "babies'" dormitory. She ran a bath for me and scrubbed me and then gave me new clothes. She threw my old clothes away – I think they went into the furnace that heated the place. They were just rags that were hanging off me. I felt so much better for it and most of all, I felt wanted.

"As I progressed, I realised what a wonderful orphanage Josiah Mason's was. Most children had at least one parent, some of whom actually paid for their children to be there. The Orphanage really was the blue riband of all institutions. I learned that the Orphanage didn't just take any children, some paid and I think some promised a legacy to the Orphanage in the hope that that would encourage a particular child to be taken in. I seem to remember that there was also an arrangement with teachers—if a teacher's child was orphaned, they would be given a place at the Orphanage. Certainly, the children who lived there cam from all over. I think maybe only about a third were from Birmingham.

"And the school had a good reputation. Children who weren't at the Orphanage came along to the school. It paid to keep in with the day boys as you might get one of the sandwiches they brought with them.

"The September after I arrived at the Orphanage, the war started. It was quiet for us for about 12 months but when the bombing started it was very frightening. The boys' dormitory was on the top floor and we were forever running down all those stairs to get to the safety of the cellar. The girls were mollycoddled on the second floor where they even had heating!

"After a time of this running up and down the stairs from the top floor to the cellar, Mr Cleaver said we might just go straight to the cellar after tea. (we were always well-fed despite rationing) Later our beds were brought down as well. After having no heating on the top floor, the cellar was lovely and warm as the furnace was in there and the cellar was so large it was possible to get lost in it..

"The noise of the gunfire and the planes was terrible but I always felt safe in the cellar. And don't forget the siren for Erdington (looked after by the Home Guard) was on the Orphanage tower. And the sound of that! It echoed all around the building. You could hear it all over the north side of Birmingham.

"In the holidays – at summer, Christmas and Easter, the Orphanage would close and we'd all be sent away. They'd give us the bus ticket or the train ticket and off we'd go on our own. Mostly we'd stay with family. I stayed with a Great Aunt.. I didn't like it: after the Orphanage, houses felt small and vulnerable in the air raids. I was terrified. Staying in the Orphanage, there were children from London, Wolverhampton, and even one boy from Glasgow, so children would travel some way for the holidays.

"I left the Orphanage in I think August 1948 when I was aged 15. It was difficult to leave because the Orphanage was what I knew. I was given a bible, my birth certificate and a ration book and I was on my way. I went into digs—the first couple were very cruel so I had to move to new digs.

"I really cannot imagine what would have happened to me if it hadn't been for Sir Josiah Mason's Orphanage. I came from the heart of Aston, the slums. I ended up going to the Technical College. Yes, there were some fights between us and I did get caned but that was just how it was. I can't say enough about what a good place it was for me.

"I went to the Council House and I saw that there were portraits of all people who have down this and that in Birmingham but I couldn't see one of Sir Josiah Mason. His picture should be there because of his Orphanage."

Memories[36]

"It was a very Dickensian place and although there were many hundreds of children who passed through those frightening doors, it was a very lonely place to be."

"Was it built for glorification? It has been suggested that it was built so large And regal so it was noticeable to all who could see it, therefore saying 'look what good I have done!'"

"Without places like this children like myself would have had little or no education, little food, and in many cases nowhere to sleep. I often wonder what would have become of me if there had not been a placement for myself. Who knows?"

"We had to wear two pairs of knickers, a navy pair and a white pair called linings."

"I remember the entrance hall being darkish and intimidating with stuffed birds etc. in glass display cases."

"The ablutions were cold and there was one bath a week which we had to share with several other girls—not at the same time though. After breakfast Mr Cleaver used to call out the names of those children who had received mail, but I was never one of them."

Life as a day pupil
Marjorie's story

"I have many happy memories of Josiah Mason School. I went in 1939 when I was nine and left in 1943. We lived in Beeches Drive and my father worked at the Dunlop Rubber Company.

"From the outside, to a young child, the Orphanage and school building looked like it was the Houses of Parliament!
"I can remember a clock tower but not the clock nor the sound it made. During World War

II, no one in England was allowed to ring church bells. We were told that if church bells rang, it meant that there was an enemy invasion. This is most probably the reason I don't recall hearing the clock chime.

"There was an enormous asphalt playground. There was also an enormous grassed field on which the newer (Yenton) school was built further down the Chester Road.

"There were four classrooms in the lower school and four in the upper school. As well as the eight classrooms we had a cookery classroom. Every alternate week we had cookery The cookery teacher was Mrs. Hudson, the other alternate week was laundry.

"There was a metal spiral staircase from the school hall to the first floor. There was also a traditional staircase at the opposite end of the building. There was a science laboratory on the second floor, reached from an extension of the spiral staircase.

"The children from the Orphanage, who were called boarders, arrived via a door in the large cloakroom near the school hall. The day children walked in the from the street down a long open air passage into the arches.

"I am almost sure the orphans had their own gardens too.

"Our school uniform was navy blue and light blue. Scarves and ties were light blue and dark blue, blazers navy with the badge on the breast pocket, and panama hats had a navy blue hat band with the badge at the front in the middle. We also had uniform P.E. kit. For the girls this was a cotton navy tunic with slits almost to the waist on either side with a wide light blue contrasting binding, with navy blue knickers.

"We didn't have school dinners, but could eat sandwiches at school. I can remember in the summer sitting on the grass in the field near Chester Road, to eat my picnic lunch. In those days we didn't get a 'lunch hour'. The break was for two hours, and I generally went home.

"For day pupils at Josiah Masons', the head master, Mr. Shillito, interviewed every pupil with their parents, and selected the best. We were tested, including reading a passage from The Birmingham Mail or The Birmingham Post, the two principal Birmingham daily newspapers, (the two other Dailies were the Birmingham Gazette and the Birmingham Despatch - considered low brow).

"Every term we had school reports. In addition to our academic progress, each one had our own age, the class average age, our own weight, the class average weight, our own height and the class average height (very time-consuming for the teachers who had no calculators in those days). I still have all my reports in the loft.

"In those days children didn't 'answer back'. They were much better behaved and obedient both at home and school. There was of course a deterrent at school for anyone who did step out of line ~ the cane. I only ever once saw a pupil being caned. A boy had 'chattered' during an air raid practice. The head master had stood on the school stage, observing the evacuation of the premises into the shelters and had observed this. When the practice was over and the pupils had returned to their classrooms, the school electric bell was rung and a school assembly was called.

"Every child in the school sat cross-legged in the large hall, staff on chairs lined one side of the hall, and prefects (also on chairs) lined the other side. The head told the head prefect to fetch his cane. The whole assemblage seemed to hold their breath. The head boy clattered all the way up the spiral staircase, his footsteps echoed along the corridor, the same happened in reverse. Then the head bellowed the name of the boy who had talked in the practice, and out he went onto the stage. In retrospect I know that the 'no speaking' rule was to avoid panic during an air raid. However, that day I was very afraid of the headmaster. He held the boy who had talked, with one hand, the cane with the other, and beat him. It was a lesson every person in that hall would always remembered. No-one ever talked on the way to or from the air raid shelters from that day onwards.

"I have given the graphic details because it was a one-off occurrence. I think I can *honestly say that my school days were really good, but that one day will always stand out in my memory.*

"Of course, as I was there during the war, I can remember frequent air raid practices and, of course, frequent air raids. I particularly remember the air raid siren at the Dunlop Rubber Company which was called the Dunlop Bull. One memory I have is of those lovely arches at the school where we could linger on hot days at playtime or lunchtime. They built air raid shelters under those arches. And we always had our gas masks with us, we never went anywhere without them.

"Children don't see differences in others the way adults do. The boarders were just other children, like us. Yes, we knew some of them had no mother or no father, or neither.

"We didn't, however, mix freely with the boarders after school. When the bell rang, they went back behind a door we were forbidden to pass through, and we went home. I can't recall any after-school activities of any description, but of course there were blackout restrictions, so we would need to hurry home."

Fort Dunlop in the days when it was the biggest tyre factory in the world.

The school: the later years

Sir Josiah gave great importance to the idea of educating the children in his orphanage. This was long before the 1880 Education Act which made formal education compulsory for all children. Even after his death, the trustees continued to spend money on the school which, after 1874 was housed in the building adjacent to the main building.

The school not only took in children from the Orphanage but also children from the local area. Former pupils describe how they had to go through an interview process to earn a place in the school. Places were highly sought after.

In 1950 management of the school was transferred from the Orphanage to Birmingham Education Department as Chester Road County Primary School. Another name change in 1952 created Yenton School (Yenton is an old name for Erdington) and a new block opened in 1954. A new infants' school building was opened a few years later completing the move out of the old school building.

> *"I went to Josiah Mason's school in the grounds of the orphanage, the 'orphans' made up about half of the pupils. The school and the orphanage were still like a Dickens novel even in the late 40s/early 50s. The school was demolished and Yenton Primary took its place."*

> *"We had to go through a large tunnel under the building to get to the playing fields at the back. I remember the entrance at the back, toilets almost opposite the door and a large staircase. My classroom was up a flight of iron stairs."*

> *"Our colours were navy and light blue. And remember the straw boaters with a ribbon around and the berets?"*[36]

Memories of the School 36

"I really hated the staircase - never felt safe on it. I remember Mr Shillito - he was nice and when we got gold stars we could go and get a toffee from a big tin he had in his room."

"I remember the iron staircase up to the classroom where we had lessons with Mrs Tharm. Also remember that the maypole was stored under the staircase and one of the boys set it on fire once which led to a caning!"

"I started school there in 1953. Not sure how long it was before the new Yenton Primary School was finished. I was terrified of the 'arches' and the cast iron staircase into the hall."

"We used to 'hide' in the arches to get out of doing our games lesson! We had

The school badge bearing the school motto 'do deeds of love' (Fac Facta Amoris) and Josiah's mermaid

some lessons in the old Orphanage classrooms too. I remember the day the main tower was demolished - we were all allowed out into the field to watch it coming down. I would have only been about eight or nine but still remember it well."

"I started my education as an infant in there before the Yenton Infants' School was opened. Some of the orphans were in my class until they moved them up to Princess Alice at New Oscott. The long corridors with stuffed birds in glass cases are still vivid memories. And the winding staircase up to the classrooms and the art room with Molly Malone's ghost... I can almost smell the paint 50+ years later."

Mason's Mermaid

The mermaid was a recurring theme in Sir Josiah's business and professional life. He chose a mermaid with a comb in her left hand and mirror in his right hand as the trademark symbol for his pen business.

The Orphanage school carried the same mermaid theme as can be seen on the school badge pictured on the previous page.

Despite the business and the school no longer existing, Sir Josiah's mermaid persists. Both the University of Birmingham and Yenton School, standing on what was once the grounds of the Orphanage, have crests incorporating the mermaid.

The idea of the mermaid appears to have come directly from the Mason family coat of arms which bore the mermaid with the comb and mirror and a lion (top right).[37]

MASON.

A mermaid statue outside the Guild of Students and, above, even a beer has taken Mason's trade mark symbol.

Above: the Yenton School badge with the mermaid from the original orphanage school badge

Below: the mermaid on the University of Birmingham crest— a nod to its beginnings as Mason's Science College

PER AD
ARDUA ALTA

Bad memories

Of course, we don't want to glorify the Orphanage. It did give shelter to many children who needed it but not everyone has good memories of their time there.

Some felt that the institution was a harsh one, others that members of staff could be cruel and punishments could be severe.

Some bad experiences and bad memories of children in care relate to specific members of staff.

Others relate to regimes which we now understand to be wrong for children. Modern approaches to tackling bed-wetting, for example, differ greatly from those of years ago when it was thought that punishing a child for wetting a bed would somehow dissuade them from doing it again.

The cane featured in many children's homes and institutions. In Birmingham, the use of the cane was banned in the early 1980s and anyone using a cane, or other such punishment on a child these days would be acting illegally.

There is no right or wrong way to remember children's homes like Mason's Orphanage. Some people have good memories, some have terrible memories and, for others, there was a mixture of good, bad and OK. Every child's experience was unique to them and, as such, there is no single way to view the Orphanage.

Simon, whose story follows, is an example of someone whose memories of the Orphanage are sadly unhappy.

Some unhappy memories of the Orphanage[36]:

"I have awful memories of the place"

"It was a very Dickensian place and although there were many hundreds of children who passed through those frightening doors, it was a very lonely place to be"

"I was an expert at making beds by the time I was five"

"I remember sitting in the dining room and dreading the moment the food would be dished up and I would be faced with another inedible meal. How I hated being there"

"We were unpaid skivvies"

"The discipline was tough and if you got out of line punishment was sometimes quite severe"

"I suffered regular nightmares about Mason's Orphanage for almost 40 years in fact. I am unsure if I benefited in any way from my time there"

"My time at the orphanage was not bad. It was at the day school where my terrors began. After the canings, the bruises on the back of my legs were black and blue"

Very hard for us all
Simon's story[38]

Simon would have been amongst the last residents of Mason's Orphanage. He arrived in 1953 and left in around 1960 shortly before it closed.

"I was seven when I went into the Orphanage and I was there eight years. My mother was a single parent and after I got run over by a milk float, two men came to our house and spoke to mum. The next thing I remember I was being taken to Josiah Mason's. There was of course no welfare assistance like there is today so I presume my mother had to go to work.

"I remember going into the building, the big doors and door bell and being met by Mr Twemlow (the Governor) and saying goodbye to my mum. Frightened and more than terrified, I hadn't a clue about how long I would be there.

"For school, I went to Yenton Infants at first, and then moved to Paget Road Secondary Modern. Other boys from the Orphanage were also there. I remember it was strange because the other pupils looked upon us being different, picked upon more but it soon settled down.

"The boys in the Orphanage were divided into two teams, Lions and Tigers, so all the sports activities were competitive between the two teams. Woe betides if you let the team down! You earned points for yourself and your team for everything that you did like smartness and creases in your trousers. We used to put our trousers under our mattresses to keep them pressed. I must admit now that is was very hard for us all. It was an Army-type regime which was not surprising considering Major Hall who ran the institution was a former officer in the Army.

"A very stern and strict man, we were all scared of Major Hall as he did many strange things. Some things were hard to understand at that age. I don't remember how many children were there - probably about a hundred.

"At first we slept in one big dormitory but later it was sectioned to incorporate several rooms each accommodating four boys. The building itself was very old and fascinating with extensive lawns and a hard playground to the rear that we could roller skate on. At the bottom of the playground there was also a large field where we used to play football and cricket, and an orchard where occasionally in the summer we would be able to eat our tea. Underneath the building itself there was an area called the arches which contained a massive laundry which could be accessed from both inside and outside the main building. I can remember that the laundry contained large boilers and dryers in order to cope with the amount of laundry necessary for the many inhabitants.
"At school holidays and Christmas those who could went home, the rest just stayed at the Orphanage. On Saturdays we were allowed to go into the local village but after one boy was caught shoplifting there was a curfew. The boy's punishment was to be beaten by the

other members of his team.

"As far as I can remember, the staff consisted of Mr and Mrs Twemlow, Major Hall, a matron, Miss Padbury who looked after the younger children and a Miss Downton. There must of course have been kitchen staff and cleaners but I didn't come into contact with them.

"I was at my happiest playing sport at which I used to excel so I could earn points for the Tigers. I also had a good voice and was made to sing during dinner which I enjoyed. On the whole because I was good at sport, always kept tidy and behaved myself I did not suffer as much as some of the other boys."

The closure of the Orphanage

The Orphanage, after 92 years, finally closed its doors in 1960. Shortly afterwards, the Orphanage was put up for sale, not as a building, but as a plot of 'valuable building land'. The land was 6.15 acres with a frontage 517 feet long. It was described in the estate agents' details as having outline planning permissions and vacant possession.

By direction of the Trustees of Sir Josiah Mason's Orphanage

ERDINGTON, BIRMINGHAM, 24

THE VERY VALUABLE

Residential Building Land

being the site of

Sir Josiah Mason's Orphanage

ORPHANAGE ROAD

(Close to Chester Road)

containing an Area of

6.15 Acres

(or thereabouts)

and having a long Frontage of about

517 FEET

OUTLINE PLANNING PERMISSIONS

VACANT POSSESSION

To be sold by Auction
At "Regent House", St Phillip's Place, Colmore Road, Birmingham, 3
On Friday, 10th JANUARY, 1964 at 2.30pm
(Subject to Prior Sale and Conditions)

By the Joint Sale Agents:

H. DONALD DIXON & COMPANY,	CHESHIRE, GIBSON & CO.
56/60 Newhall Street,	21, Waterloo Street,
Birmingham, 3.	Birmingham, 2.
Telephone: CENtral 9321.	*Telephone: MIDland 9351.*

Solicitors:
Messrs. JOHNSON & CO., 87 Cornwall Street, 3. Telephone: CENtral 7878.

It was put up for sale by auction on 10th January 1964 at Regent House in Colmore Row. The proceeds of the sale went to the trustees of the Orphanage whose charitable work in Birmingham is continued through the Sir Josiah Mason Trust.

Soon after the sale, the buildings were demolished. On the site is now a large area of housing including the new roads of Goodison Gardens and Woodway.

The Orphanage standing empty in 1964

Photograph by Phyllis Nicklin
© University of Birmingham

In readiness for the sale and redevelopment of the land, on 25th September 1961 there was issued a 'Notice of intended removal of human remains and monuments or tombstones from the burial ground and mausoleum at Sir Josiah Mason's Orphanage'[39]. The bodies were cremated and re-interred at the crematorium in Perry Barr in 1962. A plaque lists Josiah and his wife, and 54 other names, children who had died while living at the Orphanage.

The plaque, currently faded, is on a wall of many other plaques in a small enclosure called 'Mason Court'. In the summer months, the enclosure is filled with red roses. It does, perhaps, lack the personal touch of the mausoleum and graveyard in the Orphanage.

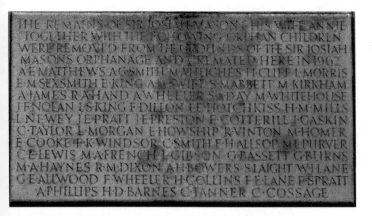

"The remains of
Sir Josiah Mason
and his wife Annie
together with the
following orphan children
were removed from the
grounds of
the Sir Josiah Mason's
Orphanage and cremated
here in 1962.

AE Matthews,
AG Smith, MA Hughes,
H Cliff, L Morris,
EM Sexsmith, E King,
AM Swift, S Mabbett,
M Kirkham, A James,
RA Hand, A Wheeler,
SA Day, M Whitehouse,
JF Nolan, LS King,
F Dillon,
LE Hotchkiss,
HM Mills, L Newey,
JE Pratt, JE Preston,
E Cotterill, J Gaskin,
C Taylor,
L Morgan,
E Howship, R Vinton,
M Homer, E Cooke,
FK Windsor, C Smith,
FH Allsop, ME Purver,
CE Lewis, MA French,
L Gibson, G Bassett,
G Burns, MA Haynes,
RM Dixon,
AH Bowers,
S Laight, WJ Lane,
GE Allwood,
F Wheeler, H Collins,
FE Lane, F Spratt,
A Phillips, HD Barnes,
C Tanner,
C Cossage"

Possible identities of those buried at the Orphanage[40]

Annie Matthews. Died 1874, aged 10.

Ada Smith. Born in Birmingham. Died 1881, aged 15.

Mary Hughes. Died 1872, aged 6.

Hannah Cliff. Died 1878, aged 13

Louisa Morris. Born in Wolverhampton. Died 1895, aged 12.

Elizabeth Sixsmith. Born in Liverpool. Died 1881, aged 15.

Elizabeth King. Born in Birmingham. Died 1881, aged 7.

Alice Swift. Died 1871, aged 12.

Sarah Mabbett. Died 1878, aged 15.

Mary Kirkham. Died 1871, aged 15.

Annie James. Died 1874, aged 10.

Rose Hand. Born in Kingswinford. Died 1881, aged 8.

Alice Wheeler. Died 1876, aged 15.

SA Day

Minnie Whitehouse. Born in Manchester. Died 1881, aged 10.

Jane Nolan. Died 1892, aged 13.

Louisa King. Died 1880, aged 9.

F Dillon

Louisa Hotchkiss. Born in Clunton. Died 1881, aged 11.

Helen Mills. Died 1876, aged 17.

Laura Newey. Died 1873, aged 14.

Julia Pratt. Died 1874, aged 19.

Jessie Preston. Died 1879, aged 11.

Emma Cotterill. Died 1871, aged 1.

Joseph Gaskin. Died 1894, aged 9.

C Taylor

Lilian Morgan. Born in Tamworth. Died 1883, aged 13.

Emily Howship. Born in Tewkesbury. Died 1881, aged 8.

Rosina Vinton. Died 1879, aged 9.

M Homer

E Cooke

Florence Windsor. Died 1883, aged 17.

Catherine Smith. Died 1876, aged 15.

Frances Allsop. Died 1886, aged 8.

Mary Purver. Died 1873, aged 13.

Clara Lewis. Born in Birmingham. Died 1881, aged 13.

Mary French. Died 1879, aged 16.

L Gibson

G Bassett

Gertrude Burns. Born in Birmingham. Died 1881 aged, 11.

Mary Haynes. Died 1874, aged 13.

Richard Dixon. Died 1889, aged 14.

Arthur Bowers. Died 1888, aged 10.

S Laight

Walter Lane. Died 1878, aged 11.

George Allwood. Died 1879, aged 12.

Frederick Wheeler. Died 1871, aged 13.

H Collins

Frederick Lane. Died 1879, aged 11.

Frank Spratt. Born in Erdington. Died 1894, aged 12.

A Phillips

Henry Barnes. Died 1876, aged 7.

C Tanner

When it came to the demolition of the largest tower of the Orphanage, workers chipped away half the base of the tower and put wooden beams in place of the bricks they removed. When they set fire to the beams, the tower collapsed amidst clouds of dust.

Memories of the demolition[36]:

> *"I was at the Yenton Infant School when they pulled it down I remember us having to hide under the desks for safety."*

> *"When they pulled down the Orphanage, my mother-in-law said that they could see what looked like the face of Josiah in the dust as the building came down."*

> *"I went to Paget Primary and we were sent outside to watch it being demolished"*

> *"I was not told that it was being closed down. I was told that I would not be going back there. Maybe they thought I was too young to understand. I wasn't upset about leaving except I missed my friends and everything I knew. I had no personal effects, no letters or photos, not even my teddy. We were not given the chance to say goodbye to anyone."*

Neighbours' memories of the Orphanage[36]:

> *"I remember playing there in the early 1960s when I was about 9 or 10 and being amazed by what I thought was an architectural wonder. It was empty at the time (probably awaiting demolition) but I thought it an amazing building and for its splendour to have such an effect on someone so young, I guess it was quite spectacular."*

> *"I remember seeing the children in the 1960s. They would all be holding hands in a crocodile and walking along very well behaved."*

> *"I remember it very well. It was huge place complete with towers and always seemed a bit frightening over all."*

Inset: a similar view in 1908 taken by Benjamin Stone, Birmingham Archives & Heritage

Reunions

The first annual reunion of people who had lived in the Orphanage was held in 1884, sixteen years after it had first opened its doors.

The matron of the time, Miss Wright arranged it on Whit Monday. Up to 200 people are thought to have attended of the 500 children who were thought to have been in the Orphanage up to that point. The Birmingham Daily Post describes the event[41]:

> *"Between 150 and 200 bygone inmates of the institutions assembled yesterday afternoon at their foster home to receive the congratulations of their former tutors and guardians. The greater proportion of the visitors came from Birmingham, but some came from as far north as Manchester and, on the south, as far as London. They were conducted over the orphanage which has undergone considerable improvement and alteration since many of them left it. Afterwards, the 'boys' were marshalled out into the adjoining meadow where they indulged in cricket and other pastimes that had been provided. After a pleasant hour in the field the visitors, with the present inmates, the latter numbering 250, partook of tea in the spacious dining room."*

One of the remarkable things about Sir Josiah Mason's Orphanage is that it is one of only a few such institutions where reunions are still regularly held. The Old Masonians' Association still runs regular get-togethers and many people find them invaluable.

Traces of Sir Josiah Mason in 21st century Erdington

Josiah Mason College was opened in 1983. In 2006 it was dissolved becoming a campus of Birmingham Metropolitan College. In 2010, it closed. This sign still stands.

Mason Cottages on Orphanage Road, now sheltered accommodation for older people, were built in 1939 on the edge of the Orphanage grounds and are managed by The Sir Josiah Mason Trust

Orphanage Road was named after the Orphanage. The name was changed from Bell Lane in the early 1900s. I have not been able to establish whether Bell Lane was named after the Orphanage's bells but it seems possible as their quarterly chimes must have been a significant feature of the road.

The one remnant of the almshouses on Station Road. This may also, of course, have been the wall of Josiah's first orphanage It used to mark the border of the almshouses, now it is around Osborne Nursery School

This road, by Erdington library, was cut in the 1880s and was given Sir Josiah's name[42]

The bust of Sir Josiah still looks towards the site where his Orphanage once stood. Now an altogether different place from the one he knew.

Acknowledgements

Particular thanks are due to:

UnLtd
Birmingham Archives and Heritage
Professor Carl Chinn
University of Birmingham
Pete Hackney

And, of course, the people who so generously gave their memories

---

References, sources and author's notes

Ref.

1. Marris, NM. (1901). *The Remarkable story of Sir Josiah Mason* in *Sunday Strand and Home* August 1901 Vol 4 No. 20

2. Annual Report of the Josiah Mason Trust, 1960. Brian Jones (Jones, B. (1985) *Josiah Mason 1795-1881 Birmingham's Benevolent Benefactor*) however, quotes a lower figure. He reports that the Orphanage was originally built to house 300 children, with almshouses for 26 women (p 60) and was enlarged in 1874 to house 300 girls and 200 boys (p 69).

3. Josiah Mason was knighted in 1872. Throughout this book, I have endeavoured to use his title when appropriate, ie. when talking of the time after 1872.

4. 1601 Poor Law Act

5. Dickens C (1838), *Oliver Twist: The Parish Boy's Progress*

6. Limbrick G. (2012). *The Children of the Homes: a century of Erdington Cottage Homes*, WordWorks, Birmingham

7. I refer to the Orphanage as Mason's Orphanage or the Orphanage throughout. However, the Orphanage also went by other names at different times including The Destitute Orphans' Home (in the early 1900s) and Sir Josiah Mason's Orphanage after he was knighted..

8. A remarkable account of Josiah's early years and career exist in the form of a biography by John Bunce, a friend of Josiah, published in 1890.

9. Curzon, MF (1997) *Erdington Methodist Church Centre Silver Jubilee 1972—1997* (unpublished)

10. Data from census returns, accessed through Ancestry.co.uk

11. Bunce, JT. (1890). *Josiah Mason—a biography*

12. *Josiah Mason's Almshouses and Orphanage at Erdington*, Birmingham Daily Post 2nd August 1869 p5

13. Marris, NM. (1901). *The remarkable story of Sir Josiah Mason* in *Sunday Strand and Home* August 1901 Vol 4 No. 20

14. *The Orphanage, Erdington*, Birmingham Gazette, 27th August 1864

15. *Josiah Mason's Almshouses and Orphanage at Erdington*, Birmingham Daily Post, 2nd August 1869 p5

16. *Visiting at the Erdington Orphanage*, Birmingham Daily Post, 17th June 1872

p5

17. *The Health of Aston Union,* Birmingham Daily Post 31st October 1894 p3

18. *The Children of the Late PC Parker,* The Preston Chronicle 27th November 1869 p6

19. *Josiah Mason's Almshouses and Orphanage at Erdington,* Birmingham Daily Post 2nd August 1869 p5

20. *Portrait No. 12 - Sir Josiah Mason* in Mid-England: a monthly magazine of Literature, Science, Art and Archaeology: Birmingham,1880, p382

21. Vincent EW & Hinton P, 1947 The University of Birmingham—its history and significance p59

22. *Bells for Mason's Orphanage,* Birmingham Gazette March 4th 1871, p5

23. http://www.hmscaptain.co.uk

24. Data is from census returns, accessed through Ancestry.co.uk

25. Data is from the Orphanage Annual reports

26. Data is from 1901 census returns, accessed through Ancestry .co.uk

27. Western, MR(2008) *Diary of an Edwardian School—Slade Road, the first 100 years*

28. *The Funeral of Sir Josiah Mason,* Birmingham Daily Post 27th June 1881 p5

29. *The late Sir Josiah Mason,* The Times, 2nd October 1885, p8

30. The Western Times, 3rd October 1871

31. This extract is from an interview carried out by P Farndon in 1997. This is not the real name of the interviewee.

33. *Radio Features,* The Nottingham Evening Post, 9th May 1927 p4

34. www.lhi.org.uk (Local Heritage Initiative)

35. Ronald Magill Obituary, The Independent 8th September 2007

Western, MR. (2008). *Diary of an Edwardian School—Slade Road, the first 100 years*

36. Many of these quotes are taken from the Mason's Orphanage Facebook page set up for this project. http://www.facebook.com/masonsorphanage Some have come from the Birmingham History Forum. http://birminghamhistory.co.uk

37. Jewitt, L. (1880) *The mermaid and the symbolism of Fish in Art, Literature and Legendary Lore,* The Reliquary Quarterly Archaeological Journal and Review Vol XX 1879—80

38. Not the contributor's real name. This was not the choice of the contributor but carried out to protect the privacy of third parties.

39. Meacham's Erdington Vol. 1 'Josiah Mason's Charity'. (Unpublished)

40. I have looked at the census returns and the birth and death records and have established that these are the possible identities of those who were buried at the Orphanage. It is, of course, impossible to be completely sure but, despite this, it felt right to attempt to give these children their identities

41. *Reunion at Sir Josiah Mason's Orphanage,* Birmingham Daily Post, 3rd June 1884

36. *A History of Birmingham on your Doorstep,* Birmingham History Forum Accessed 12/3/2011

Picture credits and sources

All photographs are from the author's own collection with the exception of the following:

Page no.

5. Mid England, 1880 p382-383

6. Wikimedia Commons

9. Dent, RK. (1880) *Old and New Birmingham: A history of the town and its people*, Houghton and Hammond, Birmingham

14. (top) Goosemoor Lane website— www.goosemoor-lane.com

16. Illustrated Midland News, 4th September 1869

17. Bunce, JT. (1890) *Josiah Mason– a biography*

18. I have drawn this plan based on the memories of people I talked to who lived in the orphanage. It is certainly not to scale and may incorporate other errors. Not all of the features shown existed at any one time.

19. Birmingham Daily Post 24th October 1881

20. Illustrated Midland News 4th September 1869

21. Illustrated Midland News 4th September 1869

23. Benjamin Stone 1908, Reproduced here with the kind permission of Birmingham Archives & Heritage

25. Illustrated Midland News, 4th September 1869

27. This photograph forms one of a series taken during demolition by someone who wishes to remain anonymous. Thanks go to Birmingham History Forum for putting us in touch with one another.

28 Painter: William F Mitchell. Source: WikiMedia Commons.

33. Benjamin Stone 1908, Reproduced here with the kind permission of Birmingham Archives & Heritage

35. Benjamin Stone 1908, Reproduced here with the kind permission of Birmingham Archives & Heritage

36. The Sunday Strand and Home, August 1901.

39. (top) The Sunday Strand and Home, August 1901.

40. Pat Evans. Reproduced here with her kind permission

44. (top) Local Heritage Initiative www.lhi.org.uk

54. Bunce, JT. (1890) *Josiah Mason– a biography*

56. Photographer Pete Hackney. Reproduced here with his kind permission

57. *The Sunday Strand and Home*, August 1901

62. as page 27

63. A mock-up of the original estate agent's auction paperwork

64. Phyllis Nicklin, Reproduced here with the kind permission of the University of Birmingham

66. (background) as page 23

70. as page 27

69. (main picture) as page 27 (inset) Benjamin Stone 1908 Birmingham Archives and Heritage

Back cover:
    Bunce, JT. (1890) *Josiah Mason– a biography*

The illustrations in this book have tended to be of the buildings rather than the children. I know that this will disappoint some people but there are two very good reasons for this. The first is that photographs of children can only be reproduced with the permission of those children and it is not always easy to trace them. The second is that ethically, it seems that the children in the orphanage deserve their privacy and dignity and should not become a public spectacle.

Index

OTHER TITLES BY THIS AUTHOR

*each based on meticulous original research
and the memories of people who spent their childhoods in the homes*

The Children of the Homes

a century of
Erdington Cottage Homes

*"Just can't put this book down!
I've spent most of the day reading -
I should be doing the decorating..."*

ISBN: 978-1-903210-28-4

How to research childhoods spent
in former children's homes,

orphanages, cottage homes
and other children's institutions

*If you are trying to find information about
a relative or distant ancestor, this is the
essential guide to where to look for records
and how to access them.*

ISBN: 978-1-903210-28-4

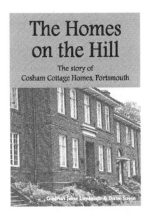

The Homes on the Hill
The story of Cosham Cottage Homes,
Portsmouth

*The cottage homes were opened in 1930 and
remained open for only 30 years. Despite their short
existence, they have witnessed terrible controversy.*

ISBN: 978-1-903210-22-2

ORDER FORM OVERLEAF

YOUR ORDER

No. of copies	Title	Price per copy
	The Children of the Homes: a century of Erdington Cottage Homes	£12.99
	Deeds of Love: The story of Josiah Mason's Orphanage	£12.99
	How to research childhoods spent in former children's homes	£8.99
	The Homes on the Hill: the story of Cosham Cottage Homes	£11.99

NAME: ....

ADDRESS: ....

....

....

....POSTCODE: ....

EMAIL: ....

Please add £1.50 for the first copy and 80p per copy for each subsequent copy for postage and packing (UK).

Total enclosed: £ ....

Please make cheques payable to **WordWorks** and send your order form to:
WORDWORKS, 120 SCHOOL RD, BIRMNGHAM B13 9TS

YOU CAN ALSO ORDER THROUGH...

www.formerchildrenshomes.org.uk/bookshop